Smart Drinks

Alcohol-Free Natural Beverages

Bob Schwiers

Sterling Publishing Co., Inc.
New York

Title-page photo and recipes *Bahamas,* page 19, and *Peppermint Drink,*
page 41: TLC-Foto-Studio GmbH, Velen-Ramsdorf
Photos on pages 56, 57: Arge Oblaten-Lebkuchen, Nuremberg;
pages 29, 49: Bacardi Deutschland GmbH, Hamburg;
page 35: Deinhard & Co. KGaA, Koblenz;
page 9: Peter Eckes AG, Nieder Olm;
pages 1, 14, 15: Henkell & Söhnlein Sektkellereien, Wiesbaden;
pages 40, 41, 57: ICE;
pages 17, 30, 31, 53: Lindavia Fruchtsaft AG, Lindau;
all other photos: Falken Archive.

Library of Congress Cataloging-in-Publication Data

Schwiers, Bob.
    [Alkoholfreie Drinks. English]
    Smart drinks : alcohol-free natural beverages / Bob Schwiers.
        p.   cm.
    Translation of Alkoholfreie Drinks.
    Includes index.
    ISBN 0-8069-9614-5
    1. Beverages.   I. Title.
TX815.S3913   1997
    641.8'75—dc20   96-38701
                                                     CIP

1   2   3   4   5   6   7   8   9   10

Published by Sterling Publishing Company, Inc.
387 Park Avenue South, New York, N.Y. 10016
Originally published in Germany under the title *Alkoholfreie Drinks*
and © 1994 by Falken-Verlag. GmbH, 65527 Niedernhausen/TS.
English translation © 1997 by Sterling Publishing Company, Inc.
Distributed in Canada by Sterling Publishing
℅ Canadian Manda Group, One Atlantic Avenue, Suite 105
Toronto, Ontario, Canada M6K 3E7
Distributed in Great Britain and Europe by Cassell PLC
Wellington House, 125 Strand, London WC2R 0BB, England
Distributed in Australia by Capricorn Link (Australia) Pty Ltd.
P.O. Box 6651, Baulkham Hills, Business Centre, NSW 2153, Australia
Printed and Bound in Hong Kong
All rights reserved

Sterling ISBN 0-8069-9614-5

Table of Contents

About This Book   4

Bar Utensils and Equipment   5

Important Mixing Ingredients   6

Light Drinks   8

Tropical Drinks   28

Milkshakes   48

Index   64

About This Book

Alcohol-free drinks are finding an ever-growing circle of friends. Smart drinks are light, fresh beverages and they offer delicious alternatives to drinks that are high in alcohol and calories. Whether fruity and thirst-quenching, tropical-exotic and smooth, spicy-aromatic and rich in vitamins, or creamy-tender and full-bodied, the variety of alcohol-free beverages is abundant!

Highballs, flips, and milkshakes without alcohol used to conjure up children's parties, but now everyone drinks these popular creations, and they can be enjoyed freely and easily. Beverage makers, aware of this, have adapted to the new trend and extended their offerings with exotic juices and syrups. With classic mixing ingredients like Curaçao Blue and cassis available alcohol-free, you can conjure up mixed drinks that appeal to the eye as well as the palate.

Mixing alcohol-free drinks has another advantage. You can purchase your basic supply of beverages inexpensively. Fruit juices and nectars, vegetable juices, and lemonades and syrups that provide aroma and color may be found in well-stocked supermarkets. You can also find supplies in specialty-food stores, health-food stores, and ethnic groceries. Items like milk, yogurt, kefir, buttermilk, and whipping cream may already be in your refrigerator. You might even be able to try many recipes in this book without going out to buy anything.

Fresh fruits and vegetables are indispensable ingredients for smart drinks. They round off the flavors and decorate your drinks. Make sure the fresh fruits you use are ripe and immaculately clean. Use only unsprayed citrus fruits, because frequently the peel is added to the drink or is used for aromatizing. And, of course, be sure to wash thoroughly any fruits or vegetables you will be using in a given recipe. This is not mentioned specifically in any recipe.

4

Abbreviations:
1 t=0.5 cl
T=tablespoon
t=teaspoon
ml=milliliter
cl=centiliter
1 cl=10 ml

l=liter
g=gram
ca.=circa
1 splash=0.1 cl
5 splashes=1 teaspoon
Recipes are measured for one person

Bar Utensils

Shaker

This bar utensil consists of a beaker, lid, and built-in strainer that holds back pieces of ice. Put the ice cubes in first, add the other ingredients, cover, and shake horizontally for 10 to 20 seconds. Strain the drink into a glass immediately, so it does not become watery. Carbonated ingredients, such as lemonade, sodas, and mineral water, should never be shaken.

Measuring Glass

Use a measuring glass for all ingredients that are easily mixed together and that must be stirred and not shaken. A measuring glass holds just over a quart (1 liter) of liquid and has a spout. Measuring glasses with integrated strainer attachments are also available.

Bar Strainer

The bar strainer is placed onto the measuring glass before the drink is poured, to hold back ice, fruit pits, and other solids.

Bar Spoon

A bar spoon holds 1 t (0.5 cl). Use it as measure and to stir the contents of the measuring glass.

Electric Blender

An electric blender or food processor is ideal for mixing drinks that contain fruits, ice cream, heavy cream, milk, or eggs. First put the ice cubes or crushed ice into the container and then add the other ingredients, cover, and blend for 10 seconds at the lowest speed and then 10 seconds at the next speed.

Glassware

Glasses are another component of the home bar. For mixed drinks, highball glasses, cocktail bowls and glasses, and tumblers are the most common. Tumblers are beaker glasses with thick glass bottoms. They are available in different sizes.

Important Mixing Ingredients

Juices

Freshly squeezed juices taste best as the basis for drinks. Premium fruit juices consist of newly harvested fresh-squeezed fruit and have nothing added. Fruit nectars are a mixture of fruit juice, fruit pulp, water, and sugar. The small, well-stocked home bar should have the following juices and nectars: pineapple, apple, apricot, grapefruit, red currant, cherry, orange, peach, grape (red and white), and lemon juice; plus banana and passion fruit nectar.

Syrups

Syrups are indispensable for the color and aroma they provide. Excellently suited for mixing are pineapple, alcohol-free cassis, alcohol-free Curaçao Blue, grenadine, strawberry, raspberry, elderberry, coconut (cream of coconut), lime, passion fruit, almond, mango, peach, lemon, and sugar syrup.

Lemonades and Water

Drinks without alcohol are unthinkable without tart lemonades and pearly mineral and soda water. These must always be well chilled. The most important fillers are bitter lemon, bitter orange, colas, ginger ale, tonic water, and taste-neutral fillers such as soda and mineral water. In addition, by using alcohol-free sparkling wines, you can mix exquisite drinks.

Ice

Nothing tastes worse than a lukewarm mixed drink. Therefore, have a lot of ice cubes in storage. If you attach great importance to crystal-clear ice cubes, boil the water before freezing it or use mineral water. When mixing drinks in a shaker, keep the ice in the shaker during straining, and pour the drink over fresh ice cubes in the glass.

Crushed Ice

Crushed ice is needed for shaking and filling. You can easily make it yourself: Wrap some ice cubes in cloth and crush them with a mallet or hammer. The crushed ice is then packed into a large glass and stored in the freezer until needed.

Fruits and Vegetables

Fruit and vegetable garnishes round off every drink optically. Any fruit or vegetable that complements the drink in taste and color is suitable to use as a decoration. Attach fruit wedges, fruit slices, fruit-peel spirals, or vegetable pieces to the rim of the glass.

LIGHT DRINKS

Fruity, low-calorie drinks are refreshing at any time of the day or night. Preparation is very simple, leaving you free to be creative.

Light Action

2 oz (6 cl) orange nectar
2½ oz (8 cl) fruit nectar
1 T (2 cl) lemon or lime juice

Garnish
1 slice of orange
1 lime slice
1 strawberry

1. Put ice cubes into a shaker and pour the nectars and juice into it.
2. Cover, shake briefly and firmly, and strain the drink over ice into a highball glass.
3. To garnish, spear the fruit with a toothpick. Place the toothpick over the rim of the glass. Serve the drink with two thick straws.
(left)

Marathon

2½ oz (8 cl) banana nectar
2 oz (6 cl) sour-cherry nectar
1½ oz (4 cl) grapefruit juice
lemon juice
2 banana slices
2 maraschino cherries
1 mint sprig

1. Shake the nectars, grapefruit juice, and ice cubes vigorously in a shaker. Strain into a highball glass.
2. Pour lemon juice on the banana slices. Spear them with a swizzle stick, alternating banana slices and cherries. Place the stick over the rim of the glass. Top with the mint.
(center)

Olympia Sprint

2 oz (6 cl) unfiltered apple juice
2 oz (6 cl) pineapple juice
2 oz (6 cl) orange juice with pulp
1 slice of orange
1 maraschino cherry
1 lime slice, 1 orange-peel spiral

1. Shake the juice and ice cubes vigorously in a shaker. Strain over ice into a highball glass.
2. Cut the orange and lime slices and the cherry and place them on the glass. Hang the orange spiral over the edge. Serve the drink with a straw.
(right)

DELICATELY TART

LIGHT   FRUITY

9

Jamaica Fruit

1 oz (3 cl) passion fruit juice
2 oz (6 cl) orange juice
2 oz (6 cl) pineapple juice
1 T (2 cl) lemon juice

Garnish
½ slice orange
1 maraschino cherry
lemon balm leaves

1. Put ice cubes into a shaker and pour the juices over them.
2. Cover, shake briefly and vigorously, and strain the drink over ice cubes into a balloon glass.
3. Spear the orange slice and cherry with a swizzle stick and attach to the rim of the glass.

TIP
Garnish this drink with a star fruit-kiwi combo. Attach a strawberry with hull, a peeled kiwi slice, a star fruit slice, and some lemon balm leaves to a long cocktail toothpick.
(*left*)

Blood-Orange

12 oz (6 cl) premium orange juice
½ T (1 cl) lemon juice
½ T (1 cl) grenadine
¼ lemon

1. Fill a highball glass half full with ice cubes.
2. Pour the juices and the grenadine over the ice. Stir thoroughly with a bar spoon.
3. Gently squeeze the lemon over the drink and then drop in the lemon.
(*center*)

Apricot Mix

3½ oz (10 cl) orange juice
3½ oz (10 cl) apricot juice
1½ oz (4 cl) lemon juice

Garnish
1 slice of orange

1. Fill a highball glass half full with ice cubes.
2. Pour the juices over it and stir with a bar spoon.
3. Cut into the orange slice to the center and attach the slice to the rim of the glass.
(right)

Bicycle

2½ oz (7 cl) mango juice
1½ oz (4 cl) lemon juice
1 T (2 cl) passion fruit juice
½ T (1 cl) grenadine
mineral water

Garnish
1 pineapple slice
1 maraschino cherry
1 small branch of lemon balm

1. Fill a highball glass halfway with ice cubes.
2. Add the juices and grenadine and stir with a bar spoon.
3. Fill glass with mineral water. Garnish with the pineapple, cherry, and lemon balm on a toothpick.
(*left*)

Sunbreaker

2½ oz (8 cl) mango juice
1 T (2 cl) lime syrup
tonic water

Garnish
1 slice of orange
1 small branch of lemon balm

1. Fill a highball glass half full with ice cubes.
2. Pour the juices over it and stir with the bar spoon.
3. Fill the glass with tonic water. Cut the orange slice halfway. Attach it and the lemon balm branch to the rim of the glass.
(*right*)

Boston Cooler

1 lemon
1 T (2 cl) grenadine
ginger ale

1. Using a citrus stripper or sharp fruit knife, peel the lemon so the skin forms a spiral.
2. Put the spiral, grenadine, and ice cubes into a highball glass. Gently mix everything with a bar spoon.
3. Fill the glass with ginger ale and serve with a thick straw.
(*left*)

American Lemonade

juice of ½ lemon
½ T (1 cl) sugar syrup
soda water

Garnish
1 slice of lemon

1. Fill a highball glass half full with ice cubes.
2. Add the lemon juice and sugar syrup and stir thoroughly with a bar spoon.
3. Fill the glass with soda water, garnish with the lemon slice, and serve with a straw.
(*right*)

13

Summer Dream

1 T (2 cl) alcohol-free Curaçao
Blue
1½ oz (4 cl) orange juice
1½ oz (4 cl) pineapple juice
3½ oz (10 cl) alcohol-free
sparkling wine, well chilled

Garnish
1 slice of orange
1 maraschino cherry

1. Fill a highball glass half full with ice cubes.
2. Pour the Curaçao and the juices over it and stir well with a bar spoon.
3. Fill the glass with the sparkling wine. Stir once lightly.
4. Place the orange slice on the rim of the glass and fasten the cherry to it with a toothpick. Serve the drink with a straw.

Strawberry Cup

2 large, ripe strawberries
1 T (2 cl) strawberry syrup
3½ oz (10 cl) alcohol-free
sparkling wine, well chilled

Garnish
1 strawberry, unbruised
1 small branch of lemon balm

1. Slice the strawberries and put them into a bowl with ice cubes.
2. Drizzle with strawberry syrup, and gently mix with the fruit and ice. Fill the glass with alcohol-free sparkling wine and stir slightly.
3. Attach the strawberry to the rim of the glass and drop the lemon balm into the drink.

Red Star

1 T (2 cl) cream of coconut
2½ oz (8 cl) sour-cherry nectar
3½ oz (10 cl) alcohol-free
sparkling wine, well-chilled

1. Put the cream of coconut and cherry nectar into a wine glass and stir thoroughly.
2. Add ice cubes and fill with the sparkling wine.

TIP

Garnish with a chunk of fresh coconut or with maraschino cherries. You can find cream of coconut in well-stocked supermarkets or in Asian groceries. Coconut cream is also available in cans in a thick liquid or a creamy solid. It is thinned with an equal volume of water before being used.

Tizian

3½ oz (10 cl) red grape juice
3½ oz (10 cl) alcohol-free
sparkling wine, well-chilled

Garnish
1 small bunch of red grapes

1. Fill a highball glass half full with ice cubes.
2. Pour the grape juice over it and fill the glass with alcohol-free sparkling wine.
3. Hang the grapes over the rim of the glass and serve the drink with a straw.

TIP

Add a splash of lemon juice to the drink to round off the taste.

15

Granizado of Lemon

½ T (1 cl) lime juice
1 T (2 cl) lemon syrup
4 T crushed ice
soda water
Garnish
1 lemon-peel spiral

1. Stir the lime juice and lemon syrup together in a large tumbler.
2. Fill a glass three-quarters full with crushed ice. Stir gently.
3. Add soda water to taste. Garnish with the lemon-peel spiral. Serve with a straw.
(facing page, top left)

Granizado of Cassis

½ T (1 cl) orange juice
1 T (2 cl) alcohol-free cassis
4 T crushed ice
soda water
Garnish
1 sprig of red currants

1. Stir the orange juice and the cassis together in a large tumbler.
2. Fill a glass three-quarters full with crushed ice and stir lightly.
3. Add soda water to taste. Place the sprig of red currants over the rim of the glass. Serve with a straw.
(facing page, top right)

Paradise

2½ oz (8 cl) passion fruit nectar
½ T (1 cl) passion fruit syrup
alcohol-free sparkling wine, well chilled

1. Put ice cubes into a shaker and pour the passion fruit nectar and syrup over it.
2. Cover, shake briefly and vigorously, and strain into a champagne glass.
3. Fill the glass slowly with alcohol-free sparkling wine. Stir gently.
(facing page, bottom)

Yellow Bird

1½ oz (4 cl) lime syrup
2½ oz (8 cl) grapefruit juice
5½ oz (16 cl) bitter lemon
Garnish
1 slice of lemon or lime

1. Put ice cubes into a shaker and add the lime syrup and grapefruit juice.
2. Cover, shake briefly and vigorously, and strain into a highball glass.
3. Slowly fill the glass with bitter lemon, stirring carefully. Attach the lemon or lime slice to the rim of the glass.

WITH LEMON SYRUP WITH CASSIS

WITH PASSION FRUIT SYRUP

El Dorado

1½ oz (4 cl) guava juice
1½ oz (4 cl) orange juice
1½ oz (4 cl) passion fruit juice
1½ oz (4 cl) pineapple juice
tonic water

Garnish
½ slice pineapple
1 slice of orange
1 green maraschino cherry

1. Put ice cubes into a shaker and add the juices.
2. Cover, shake briefly and vigorously, and strain into a highball glass.
3. Fill with tonic water and stir lightly. Garnish with the fruit.
(*left*)

Pear Cocktail

1½ oz (4 cl) pear juice
1½ oz (4 cl) apricot juice
1½ oz (4 cl) kiwi-citrus juice
1½ oz (4 cl) orange juice

Garnish
1 kiwi slice
1 small canned pear
1 slice of orange

1. Put ice cubes into a mixing glass.
2. Add the juices, stir with a bar spoon, and strain into a highball glass.
3. Spear the fruits with a swizzle stick and place the stick over the rim of the glass.
(*right*)

18

William Tell's Shot

3½ oz (10 cl) apple juice
1½ oz (5 cl) grapefruit juice
1 T (2 cl) lemon juice
½ T (1 cl) grenadine
2 splashes of almond syrup

Garnish
1 canned crab apple

1. Put ice cubes into a shaker. Add the juices and the syrups.
2. Cover, shake briefly and vigorously, and strain into a highball glass filled with ice cubes.
3. Spear the crab apple with a swizzle stick. Garnish the drink with it. (*left*)

Bahamas

1½ oz (5 cl) apple juice
1 T (2 cl) lemon juice
½ T (1 cl) grenadine

Garnish
1 slice of star fruit

1. Fill a highball glass half full with ice cubes.
2. Add the juices and the grenadine. Stir with a bar spoon.
3. Cut the slice of star fruit halfway and attach it to the rim of the glass. (*right*)

Pirate's Fire

1½ oz (4 cl) apricot juice
1½ oz (4 cl) pear juice
1 T (2 cl) cherry juice
1 T (2 cl) lemon juice
½ T (1 cl) grenadine
tonic water

Garnish
1 lemon-peel spiral
1 maraschino cherry

1. Put ice cubes into a shaker and add the juices and grenadine.
2. Cover; shake briefly and vigorously, and strain into a highball glass.
3. Add tonic water to taste.
4. Drape the lemon-peel spiral over the rim of the glass. Spear the maraschino cherry with a cocktail toothpick and place it in the drink. (*left*)

Saratoga Cooler

1 T (2 cl) grenadine
1 T (2 cl) lemon juice
ginger ale

Garnish
1 lemon slice
1 slice of orange
1 maraschino cherry

1. Stir the grenadine and the lemon juice in a tumbler.
2. Fill the glass with ginger ale and decorate it with the fruits.

TIP
To vary this drink, put 1 T of mixed berries (blackberries, raspberries, or blueberries) in the glass.
(*center*)

Lemon Squash

juice of ½ lemon or lime
1 t confectioners' sugar
soda water

Garnish
2 slices of lemon

1. Stir the lemon juice and the confectioners' sugar in a tumbler.
2. Add ice cubes, stir again, and fill the glass with soda water, to taste.
3. Add the lemon slices to the glass. Serve with a bar spoon and straw.

TIP
When preparing drinks, always mix the sugar with the other ingredients before adding ice. Sugar dissolves poorly at low temperatures.
(*right*)

Tonic Fresh

2 oz (6 cl) orange juice
1 oz (3 cl) pineapple juice
1 T (2 cl) lemon juice
1 T (2 cl) raspberry syrup
tonic water

Garnish
1 lemon-peel spiral

1. Put ice cubes into a shaker. Add the juices and the syrup.
2. Cover, shake briefly and vigorously, and strain into a highball glass with ice cubes.
3. Fill the glass with tonic water. Stir once briefly. Drape the lemon spiral over the rim of the glass.

Cherry Kiss

3 oz (9 cl) cherry juice
1½ oz (5 cl) pineapple juice
1 oz (3 cl) lemon juice
1 T (2 cl) cherry syrup

Garnish
1 cocktail cherry
½ slice pineapple

1. Put ice cubes into a shaker and add the juices and syrup.
2. Cover, shake briefly and vigorously, and strain into a highball glass filled with ice cubes.
3. Spear the cherry and the pineapple slices with a toothpick and attach to the rim of the glass.

Citro Fizz

10 ice cubes
½ T (1 cl) lemon juice
soda water
2 T (4 cl) lemon syrup
1 T (2 cl) grenadine
soda water

Garnish
1 slice of lemon

1. Put half the ice cubes into a shaker and add the lemon juice, syrup, and grenadine.
2. Cover, shake briefly and vigorously, and strain into a highball glass.
3. Fill the glass with soda water and stir again. Add the balance of the ice cubes. Attach the lemon slice to the rim of the glass.

Orange Fizz

1 T (2 cl) grenadine
1 T (2 cl) raspberry juice
½ T (1 cl) orange juice
4 ice cubes
tonic water

Garnish
1 slice of orange

1. Put the ice cubes into a shaker. Add the grenadine and juices.
2. Cover, shake briefly and vigorously, and strain into a highball glass.
3. Fill the glass with tonic water and stir again. Attach the orange slice to the rim of the glass.

Exotic Cup

1½ oz (5 cl) pineapple juice
1 oz (3 cl) mango juice
1 T (2 cl) passion fruit juice
1 T (2 cl) cream of coconut
½ T (1 cl) lemon juice
½ T (1 cl) grenadine
mineral water

Garnish
¼ slice pineapple
1 maraschino cherry

1. Put ice cubes into a measuring glass.
2. Pour the juices, cream of coconut, and grenadine over it and stir with the bar spoon.
3. Strain the drink into a highball glass and fill it with mineral water.
4. Spear the pineapple slice and the cherry with a cocktail toothpick and attach them to the rim of the glass.

TIP
Summer drinks are more refreshing when they are served in pre-cooled glasses. Place glasses in the freezer and leave them until they are covered with a film of ice.
(*left*)

Blushing Virgin

2 scoops of vanilla ice cream
juice of 2 blood-oranges
5 oz (125 ml) soda water, well chilled

Garnish
1 orange-peel spiral

1. Put the vanilla ice cream into a highball glass.
2. Add the orange juice and fill the glass with soda water.
3. Drape the orange-peel spiral over the rim of the glass.
(*center*)

Big Apple

2 apple juice ice cubes
3 oz (9 cl) grenadine
2 oz (6 cl) orange juice
1½ oz (4 cl) apple juice
soda water

Garnish
1 canned crab apple

1. Mix the apple juice ice cubes, grenadine, and juices in a measuring glass.
2. Pour the drink into a highball glass and fill it with soda water.
3. Cut the crab apple halfway through and attach it to the rim of the glass.
(*right*)

Virgin Mary

7 oz (20 cl) tomato juice
1 splash of lemon juice
salt & freshly ground pepper
1 splash of Worcestershire sauce
1 splash of Tabasco
1 celery stalk

1. Put ice cubes into a measuring glass. Add the juices and stir thoroughly. Add the seasonings and strain over a tumbler.
2. Garnish with the celery stalk. (*left*)

Tomato Cress

2 oz (6 cl) tomato juice
1 T (2 cl) crème fraîche
fresh cress

1. Stir the tomato juice, crème fraîche, and ice in a measuring glass.
2. Strain over ice cubes into a cocktail bowl and garnish with cress. (*center*)

Carlotta

1½   oz (4 cl) celery juice
1½   oz (4 cl) carrot juice
1½   oz (4 cl) apple juice
1 splash of lemon juice
1 t chopped parsley

1. Mix the juice and ice cubes. Strain into a highball glass.
2. Sprinkle with parsley. (*right*)

Power Juice

3½ oz (10 cl) red beet juice
3½ oz (10 cl) carrot juice
1 T (2 cl) lemon juice
 freshly ground black pepper

Garnish
1 long, narrow piece of cucumber

1. Put ice cubes into a tumbler and add the juices.
2. Stir well with the bar spoon. Add pepper, to taste.
3. Decorate the drink with the cucumber.
(*left*)

Bavarian Tomato

3½ oz (10 cl) tomato juice
3½ oz (10 cl) sauerkraut juice
1 t ground caraway seeds

Garnish
1 celery stalk
1 cherry tomato
freshly ground black pepper

1. Put ice cubes into a shaker. Add the juices and caraway seeds.
2. Cover, shake briefly and vigorously, and pour into a highball glass.
3. Garnish with the celery stalk and the cherry tomato. Sprinkle the drink with black pepper.
(*right*)

27

TROPICAL DRINKS

Don't assume tropical drinks must have rum. You'll be amazed at what delicious Pacific Ocean dreams can be mixed without alcohol!

Tropical

1½ oz (5 cl) orange juice
1½ oz (5 cl) mango juice
1½ oz (5 cl) pineapple juice
½ T (1 cl) lemon juice
½ T (1 cl) grenadine

Garnish
pineapple wedge

1. Put ice cubes into a measuring glass
2. Add the juices and grenadine and stir well with a bar spoon.
3. Strain into a highball glass and garnish with the pineapple wedge. (*left*)

Miami

4½ oz (14 cl)) pineapple juice
½ T (1 cl) lemon juice
½ T (1 cl) sugar syrup
½ T (1 cl) peppermint syrup

Garnish
1 slice of lemon
1 small mint sprig

1. Put ice cubes into a shaker and add the juices and syrups.
2. Cover, shake briefly and vigorously, and strain into a highball glass.
3. Cut the lemon slice to the middle. Attach it and the mint sprig to the rim of the glass. (*center*)

Limbo Beat

1½ oz (5 cl) banana syrup
1 T (2 cl) lemon juice
bitter orange

1. Fill a highball glass half full with ice cubes.
2. Add the banana syrup and lemon juice and stir well with a bar spoon.
3. Fill with bitter orange.
(*right*)

WITH BANANA SYRUP

WITH PEPPERMINT SYRUP

WITH EXOTIC FRUIT JUICES

Caribic

1 small pineapple
4 oz (12 cl) multi-vitamin fruit
nectar
1½ oz (4 cl) grenadine

Garnish
1 slice of an untreated orange

1. With a sharp knife, cut the lid off the pineapple. Cutting along the inside edge of the skin, carefully remove a large, round section of pineapple. Remove any tough, woody parts and cut the pineapple into small pieces.

2. Put about a tablespoon of pineapple bits in the hollow shell, set some aside for the garnish, and save the remainder for something else.

3. Shake the fruit nectar and grenadine well with ice cubes in a shaker and strain into the pineapple. Fill with crushed ice.

4. Garnish the drink with a swizzle stick decorated with the orange slice and pineapple pieces.

TIP
Serve the Caribic on a dessert plate with a teaspoon and napkin. Mixed drinks that are garnished extravagantly should be served on small plates or napkins so the swizzle sticks, toothpicks, and fruit skins can be discarded onto them.

Tropical Fire

3½ oz (10 cl) passion fruit nectar
1½ oz (5 cl) peach nectar
½ T (1 cl) lemon juice
½ T (1 cl) peach syrup

Garnish
2 peach slices

1. Put ice cubes into a shaker and add the nectars, juice, and syrup.
2. Cover, shake briefly and vigorously, and strain into a highball glass.
3. Fill with crushed ice. Garnish with peach wedges on a cocktail toothpick.
(*top*)

Red Butler

3½ oz (10 cl) blood-orange nectar
3½ oz (10 cl) alcohol-free Italian bitters

Garnish
1 untreated orange-peel spiral

1. Fill a highball glass half full with ice cubes.
2. Add the nectar and bitters and slowly stir with the bar spoon.
3. Add the orange spiral to the glass.

Pineapple Freeze

2 oz (6 cl) pineapple syrup
3–4 T crushed ice
1 scoop pineapple ice cream
soda water

Garnish
½ slice of pineapple

1. Put the pineapple syrup into a large highball glass.
2. Fill the glass two-thirds full with crushed ice. Add the pineapple ice cream.
3. Fill the drink with soda water, garnish with the pineapple, and serve with a bar spoon.
(*left*)

Berry Freeze

1 oz (3 cl) alcohol-free cassis
1 scoop of red currant ice cream or sorbet
4 T crushed ice
soda water

Garnish
1 bunch of red currants

1. Pour the cassis into a large highball glass.
2. Fill the glass two-thirds full with crushed ice and add the red currant ice cream or sorbet.
3. Fill the glass with soda water and garnish with the berries. Serve with a bar spoon and a straw.
(*center*)

Passion Fruit Freeze

½ T (1 cl) raspberry or elderberry syrup
½ T (1 cl) lemon juice
2½ oz (8 cl) passion fruit juice
soda water

Garnish
1 maraschino cherry

1. Put ice cubes into a shaker and add the syrup and the juices to it.
2. Cover, shake briefly and vigorously, and strain into a champagne flute.
3. Fill the glass with soda water, spear the cherry with a cocktail toothpick, and place it in the drink.
TIP
Make fruit ice cream yourself. It's very simple. For 5 servings, you need 130 g strained fruit pulp, 4 oz (12 cl) mineral water, 1 egg white, and 50 g sugar. Mix the fruit pulp and mineral water. Whip the egg white and sugar until stiff peaks form, add to the fruit mix, and freeze.
(*right*)

Samoa

½ T (1 cl) lime syrup
½ T (1 cl) alcohol-free Curaçao
 Blue
1 oz (3 cl) passion fruit nectar
2 oz (6 cl) tropical fruit juice mix

1. Put ice cubes into a shaker and
add all the ingredients .
2. Cover and shake briefly and vigorously.
3. Strain into a highball glass.
TIP
Garnish the drink with nectarines
and orange slices.
(*left*)

Sunny Coco

1 oz (3 cl) peach nectar
1 oz (3 cl) coconut cream
1½ oz (4 cl) orange juice with
 fruit pulp
1½ oz (5 cl) pineapple juice

1. Put ice cubes into a shaker and
add the ingredients.
2. Cover and shake briefly and vigorously.
3. Strain into a cocktail glass and
serve with a straw.
(*left*)

Balear

1½ oz (4 cl) pineapple juice
1 T (2 cl) mango juice
1 T (2 cl) banana syrup
2 oz (6 cl) tropical fruit juice mix

1. Put ice cubes into a shaker and
add all the ingredients.
2. Cover and shake briefly and vigorously.
3. Strain into a highball glass.
TIP
Decorate this drink with a cocktail
toothpick speared with banana and
pineapple slices.
(*right*)

Pyramid

1 T (2 cl) mango syrup
½ T (1 cl) lime syrup
1 T (2 cl) apricot nectar
2 oz (6 cl) orange juice with fruit
 pulp

1. Put ice cubes into a shaker and
add all the ingredients over them.
2. Cover and shake briefly and vigorously.
3. Strain into a cocktail glass and
serve with a straw.
(*right*)

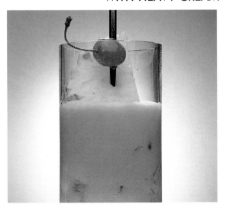 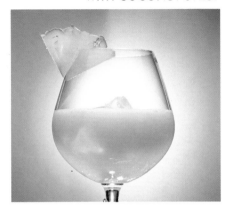

Pink Dune

7 oz (20 cl) pineapple juice
1 T (2 cl) heavy cream
½ T (1 cl) grenadine

Garnish
½ slice pineapple
1 maraschino cherry

1. Put ice cubes into a shaker and add the juice, cream, and syrup.
2. Cover, shake briefly and vigorously, and strain into a highball glass.
3. Fill with crushed ice. Spear the fruit with a cocktail toothpick and put it into the drink.

L'Arbre du Ciel

1½ oz (4 cl) coconut syrup
2 oz (6 cl) pineapple syrup
1 T (2 cl) lemon juice
¼ t shredded coconut

Garnish
¼ slice pineapple

1. Put ice cubes into a shaker and add the syrups, juice, and coconut.
2. Cover, shake briefly and vigorously, and strain into a red wine glass.
3. Attach the pineapple slice to the rim of the glass.

36

Coconut-Cream Soda

2 scoops of coconut ice cream
1½ oz (4 cl) coconut milk
1½ oz (4 cl) pineapple juice
1 t cream of coconut
2 splashes of lemon juice
soda water

1. Put ice cubes into a shaker and add all the ingredients except the soda water.
2. Cover, shake briefly and vigorously, and strain into a highball glass.
3. Fill the drink to taste with soda water and stir briefly.

Coco Exotic

1½ oz (4 cl) mango juice
1 T (2 cl) peach juice
½ T (1 cl) passion fruit juice
1 oz (3 cl) pineapple juice
2 oz (6 cl) cream of coconut
½ T (1 cl) heavy cream
mineral water

Garnish
1 mango slice

1. Put ice cubes into a shaker and add the juices and creams.
2. Cover, shake briefly and vigorously, and strain into a highball glass.
3. Fill to taste with mineral water and decorate with the mango slice.

Apricot Fizz

½ T (1 cl) freshly squeezed
  orange juice
½ T (1 cl) freshly squeezed
  lemon juice
2 oz (6 cl) apricot juice
ice-cold soda water

Garnish
½ apricot

1. Put ice cubes into a shaker and add the juices.
2. Cover, shake briefly and vigorously, and strain into a highball glass.
3. Fill to taste with soda water. Attach the apricot half to the rim of the glass. Serve with a straw.
(*left*)

Pincasso

½ T (1 cl) bitter lemon
½ T (1 cl) grenadine
1 T (2 cl) lime juice
1½ oz (4 cl) grapefruit juice
1½ oz (5 cl) red grape juice
ice-cold soda water

Garnish
1 sprig of lemon balm

1. Put ice cubes into a shaker. Add the bitter lemon, grenadine, and juices.

2. Cover, shake briefly and vigorously, and strain into a highball glass.
3. Add the lemon balm to the glass and serve the drink with a straw.
(*right*)

Pineapple Fizz

½ T (1 cl) lemon juice
2 oz (6 cl) pineapple juice
1 drop Worcestershire sauce
ice-cold soda water

Garnish
¼ baby pineapple

1. Put ice cubes into a shaker and add the juices and seasoning.
2. Cover, shake briefly and vigorously, and strain into a highball glass.
3. Carefully slide the pineapple into the glass. Serve the drink on a small plate with a straw.

Avalanche

1 untreated lime
1 scoop of lemon ice cream or
** sorbet**
bitter lemon

Garnish
1 lime slice

1. Grate the lime skin and squeeze out the juice. Combine the skin, juice, and ice cream or sorbet in a tall glass.
2. Slowly and carefully fill the glass three-quarters full with bitter lemon, letting the foam settle before continuing to pour. Cut the lime slice and attach it to the rim of the glass. Serve with a bar spoon.
(*top*)

Red Cap

1 T fresh raspberries
½ T (1 cl) raspberry syrup
1 scoop of raspberry ice cream
soda water

Garnish
1 unbruised raspberry
1 small mint sprig

1. Puree the raspberries. Combine the puree and syrup in a highball glass.
2. Slide the ice cream into the glass and fill with soda water.
3. Attach the raspberry and the mint to the rim of the glass. Serve with a bar spoon.

Peppermint Drink

5 oz (150 ml) ice-cold pepper-
mint tea
½ T (1 cl) peppermint syrup
1 t sugar
1 scoop strawberry ice cream or
sorbet

Garnish
1 lime slice
1 maraschino cherry
1 small mint sprig

1. Put some ice cubes into a measuring glass.
2. Add the tea, syrup and sugar; stir with a bar spoon; and strain into a highball glass.

3. Let the strawberry ice cream or sorbet slide into the glass, and garnish the drink with the fruit and mint. Serve with a small spoon.

TIP
Use fresh peppermint leaves, so the drink tastes even more intense. Pour boiling water over 1 teaspoon of fresh peppermint leaves and let the tea steep for about 10 minutes.

41

Orange Lemonade

1½ oz (5 cl) orange juice
1 T (2 cl) lemon juice
1 T (2 cl) sugar syrup
soda water

Garnish
1 slice of orange

1. Put ice cubes into a tumbler.
2. Add the juices and syrup and stir thoroughly with the bar spoon.
3. Fill the glass with soda water and attach the orange slice to the rim of the glass.
(*top*)

Strawberry Plant

2 large fresh strawberries
2 oz (6 cl) orange juice
2 oz (6 cl) pineapple juice
1 oz (3 cl) lemon juice
1 T (2 cl) strawberry syrup

1. In an electric blender, puree the strawberries, juices, and syrup.
2. Pour the drink over ice cubes into a highball glass.
(*bottom left*)

Orange Fresh

2 oz (6 cl) orange juice
1 T (2 cl) lemon juice
1 T (2 cl) pineapple juice
1 scoop lemon ice cream or
  sorbet
ginger ale

Garnish
1 slice of orange

1. Mix the juices in a highball glass with the bar spoon.
2. Let the lemon ice cream or sorbet slide into the glass and fill the drink with ginger ale.
3. Attach the orange slice to the rim of the glass.

Mississippi

2½ oz (8 cl) alcohol-free crème de cassis
2½ oz (8 cl) orange juice

Garnish
1 slice of orange

1. Put ice cubes into a tumbler.
2. Add the crème de cassis and orange juice and stir well.
3. Cut the orange slice to the center and put it on the rim of the glass.

TIP
For a sweeter taste, substitute black currant juice for the orange juice. Add two tablespoons of crushed ice to the glass to dilute it.
(*bottom right*)

Babouin

½   T (1 cl) orange juice
1 T (2 cl) lime juice
1 oz (3 cl) pineapple juice
1½   oz (4 cl) passion fruit juice
2 oz (5 cl) cherry juice

Garnish
½   peeled banana
pineapple bits
2 maraschino cherries

1. Put ice cubes into a shaker and add the juices.
2. Cover, shake, and strain into a highball glass.
3. Cut the banana into slices and put them, the pineapple bits, and the cocktail cherries into the glass.
4. Serve with a bar spoon. (*left*)

Coconut Cocktail

½   T (1.5 cl) grenadine
½   T (1.5 cl) lemon juice
1 t cream of coconut
½   T (1.5 cl) passion fruit juice
1½   oz (4 cl) pineapple juice
1½   oz (4 cl) coconut milk

Garnish
1 mint sprig

1. Put ice cubes into a shaker and pour the ingredients over them.
2. Cover, shake briefly and vigorously, and strain into a cocktail glass.
3. Decorate with the mint sprig. (*right*)

Raspberry Cocktail

2 oz (50 g) raspberries
1 t sugar
½ T (1 cl) lemon juice
1 T (2 cl) orange juice
scooped-out vanilla pulp
1 scoop of raspberry sorbet

Garnish
2 lemon-peel spirals

1. Mix the raspberries and sugar and leave the mix for about 1 hour.
2. In a blender, puree the raspberries, juice, vanilla pulp, and sorbet.
3. Shake vigorously with ice cubes in a shaker. Strain into a glass.
4. Decorate the glass with the lemon-peel spirals.
(*left*)

Sunrise

1 t grenadine
½   T (1 cl) lemon juice
1 T (2 cl) grapefruit juice
5 oz (15 cl) orange juice

Garnish
1 slice of an untreated orange

1. Put ice cubes into a shaker and add the juices.
2. Cover, shake briefly and vigorously, and strain into a highball glass.
3. Attach the orange slice to the rim of the glass.
(*right*)

45

Banana Soda

2 scoops of vanilla ice cream
3½ oz (10 cl) banana juice
½ T (1 cl) lemon juice
soda water

1. Mix the vanilla ice cream with the juices in a highball glass.
2. Fill the drink with soda water and stir again.
(*background left*)

Sweet Susie

1 scoop of vanilla ice cream
1 scoop of pineapple ice cream
1 T (2 cl) raspberry juice
soda water

Garnish
whipped cream
2 strawberries

1. Put the ice cream and the raspberry juice into a tumbler.
2. Fill the glass with soda water and stir.
3. Add whipped cream and top with strawberries. Serve with a spoon.
(*front left*)

Triver

2 oz (5 cl) passion fruit juice
1½ oz (4 cl) peach juice
1 oz (3 cl) cream of coconut
1 T (2 cl) lemon juice
mineral water

Garnish
1 kiwi slice
1 maraschino cherry

1. Put ice cubes, juices, and cream of coconut in a shaker.
2. Cover, shake briefly and vigorously, and strain into a highball glass.
3. Fill with mineral water and stir briefly.
4. Attach the kiwi slice to the rim and fasten the cherry onto it.
(*background, right*)

Strawberry Soda

1 scoop of strawberry ice cream
1 T (2 cl) lemon juice
1 T (2 cl) strawberry syrup
soda water

1. Put the ice cream, lemon juice, strawberry syrup, and ice cubes into a shaker.
2. Cover, shake briefly and vigorously, and strain into a tumbler.
3. Fill with soda water and stir briefly.
(*front right*)

MILKSHAKES

Not just for children, creamy-smooth shakes may contain fruit, ice cream, or egg yolks. Milk products are great for alcohol-free drinks.

Strawberry Milkshake

6–8 fresh strawberries
4 oz (12 cl) milk
3 t confectioners' sugar
1 scoop strawberry ice cream

Garnish
1 T whipped cream
1 large strawberry

1. Free the strawberries from the hulls, halve them, and mix them thoroughly in a food processor with the milk, sugar, and ice cream.
2. Pour the shake into a goblet, decorate with whipped cream, and garnish with a strawberry.
3. Serve with a straw and a spoon.
TIP
Vary this recipe by using peaches, bananas, or pineapples.
(*left*)

Orange Milkshake

2 oz (60 ml) orange juice
grated peel of half an orange
1 T (2 cl) almond syrup
1 scoop of vanilla ice cream
1 t confectioners' sugar
4 oz (12 cl) milk

Garnish
½ t chocolate shavings

1. Put all the ingredients except the garnish into a food processor and combine.
2. Pour into a champagne glass and sprinkle with chocolate shavings.
(*center*)

Blue Moon

1 T (2 cl) alcohol-free Curaçao Blue
1 scoop of vanilla ice cream
1 T (2 cl) heavy cream
3½ oz (10 cl) milk

Garnish
1 mint sprig

1. Put the Curaçao, ice cream, cream and milk into a food processor and combine.
2. Pour the shake into a champagne glass and garnish with the mint.
(*right*)

WITH CURAÇAO

CREAMY

WITH ALMOND SYRUP

Banana Mix

½ banana
juice of ½ orange
1 t sugar
½ t vanilla sugar
4 oz (12 cl) buttermilk

Garnish
1 slice of an untreated orange

1. Slice the banana half. Thoroughly combine it in the food processor with the orange, sugars, and buttermilk.
2. Pour into a highball glass and garnish with the orange slice.
(*far left*)

Sonny Boy

1 small egg yolk
1 t grape sugar
juice of 1 orange
3½ oz (100 g) kefir

1. Put everything into a food processor and combine thoroughly.
2. Pour into a highball glass and serve.
(*foreground, right*)

Tropical Sun

5 oz (150 ml) mango, cut into cubes
1 t sugar
4 oz (12 cl) buttermilk

Garnish
1 mint sprig

1. Put the mango, sugar, and buttermilk into a food processor and combine thoroughly.
2. Pour into a cocktail glass and garnish with the mint.
(*background, left*)

Apricot-Kefir Drink

2½ oz (75 g) pureed apricots
1 t sugar
½ t vanilla sugar
1 oz (3 cl) orange juice
4½ oz (125 g) kefir

Garnish
1 slice of an untreated orange
1 sprig of lemon balm

1. Put everyting except the garnish into a food processor and combine thoroughly.
2. Pour into a highball glass.
3. Attach the orange slice to the rim of the glass and fasten the lemon balm to it. Serve with a straw.
(*far right*)

Vitamin Milk

3½ oz (10 cl) multi-vitamin juice
3½ oz (10 cl) ice-cold milk
1 T (2 cl) lemon juice

Garnish
1 T lightly whipped heavy cream
lemon balm leaves

1. Thoroughly combine the multi-vitamin juice and the milk in a food processor.
2. Pour into a highball glass and sprinkle with lemon juice.
3. Decorate with whipped cream, sprinkle with lemon balm leaves, and serve with a straw.
(*top*)

B-Vitamin Milkshake

4 oz (12 cl) multi-vitamin drink
3½ oz (10 cl) ice-cold milk
1 T (2 cl) grenadine

Garnish
1 slice of an untreated apple

1. Put ice cubes into a shaker and add the B-vitamin drink, milk, and grenadine.
2. Cover and shake briefly and vigorously.
3. Strain the drink into a highball glass and garnish with the apple-slice.
(*bottom*)

Citronella

1 scoop lemon ice cream
½ T (1 cl) lemon juice
1 t sugar
4 oz (12 cl) buttermilk

Garnish
1 slice of an untreated lemon
1 lemon-peel spiral

1. Put the ice cream, juice, sugar, and buttermilk in a food processor and combine thoroughly.
2. Pour into a highball glass.
3. Attach the lemon slice to the rim of the glass and hang the spiral over the rim too.

Kiba

1½ oz (5 cl) cherry juice
1½ oz (5 cl) banana juice
1 splash of lemon juice
3½ oz (10 cl) ice-cold buttermilk

Garnish
banana slices

1. Put the juices and buttermilk in a food processor and combine thoroughly.
2. Pour into a highball glass.
3. Spear the banana slices with a cocktail toothpick and place it over the edge of the glass.

Cola-Mint Cream

1½ oz (5 cl) heavy cream
1 oz (3 cl) chocolate syrup
½ T (1 cl) peppermint syrup
cola

Garnish
1 mint sprig

1. Put ice cubes into a shaker and add the heavy cream and syrups.
2. Cover, shake briefly and vigorously, strain into the tumbler, and fill with cola.
3. Attach the mint to the rim and serve with a straw.
(*left*)

Chocolate-Orange Drink

2 scoops of vanilla ice cream
1 T (2 cl) chocolate syrup
1 T (2 cl) orange syrup
well-chilled milk

Garnish
1 T stiffly whipped cream
1 orange slice
chocolate shavings

1. In a tumbler, whisk the ice cream and syrups lightly.
2. Fill with milk, decorate with whipped cream, and place the slice of orange on the edge of the glass.
3. Finally, sprinkle the drink with chocolate shavings and serve immediately with a bar spoon.
(*right*)

Coco Almond

1½ oz (5 cl) cream of coconut
1½ oz (5 cl) almond syrup
1 splash of grenadine
well-chilled milk

1. Put plenty of ice into a shaker and add all the ingredients except the milk.
2. Cover, shake briefly and vigorously, and strain into a highball glass.
3. Fill the glass with milk and serve with a straw.
(*left*)

Red Currant Creamy

1 scoop of red currant ice cream
1½ oz (5 cl) red currant syrup
1 T (2 cl) cherry juice
well-chilled milk
2 oz (50 g) red currants

Garnish
1 bunch of red currants

1. Put the ice cream into a tumbler, and add the syrup and juice. Stir.
2. Fill the glass with milk and add the berries.
3. Garnish with the red currants and serve with a teaspoon.
(*right*)

Vitamin Bomb

¼ **papaya**
¼ **avocado**
3½ **oz (100 g) strawberry halves**
1 T sugar
2 scoops of vanilla ice cream
ice-cold milk

1. Put the papaya, avocado, and strawberries in the food processor and puree.
2. Add the sugar and the ice cream and beat vigorously.
3. Fill with milk to the ½ liter level and mix well once again .
4. Serve in a large glass with a straw.
TIP
You can replace the papaya with a ripe nectarine.

Red Currant Flip

1 oz (3 cl) red currant juice
5 oz (150 ml) well-chilled milk
1 egg yolk
vanilla ice cream on a stick
Garnish
cocoa

1. Put ice cubes into a shaker. Add the red currant juice, milk, and egg yolk, and shake briefly and vigorously.
2. Set the ice cream bar into a wide glass and strain the milk-mixture over it.
3. Dust with cocoa.
TIP
Vary the Red Currant Flip by adding 1 T (2 cl) of alcohol-free cassis.

Magic Drink

2 t sugar
7 oz (20 cl) milk
⅛ t cinnamon

Garnish
1 T stiffly beaten whipped cream
crushed nuts

1. Melt the sugar in a pot until it becomes light brown. Pour milk over it and stir at low heat until the caramelized sugar has completely dissolved.
2. Season the caramel-milk with cinnamon powder, let cool a bit, and pour into a heat-resistant glass.
3. Decorate with whipped cream and sprinkle with crushed nuts.

Chocolate-Nut Milk

8 oz (24 cl) milk
1 t nougat cream
1 t maple syrup
⅛ t cinnamon

Garnish
1 T stiffly beaten whipped cream
chocolate sprinkles

1. Heat the milk. Dissolve the nougat cream in it and stir in the maple syrup and cinnamon.
2. Pour into a heat-resistant glass.
3. Cover with whipped cream and top with chocolate sprinkles.

57

Grape Egg Nog

2½ oz (8 cl) red grape juice
2½ oz (8 cl) milk
½ T (1 cl) sugar syrup
1 egg yolk

1. Put ice cubes into a shaker and add all ingredients.
2. Cover, shake briefly, and strain into a highball glass.

TIP

You can also prepare this drink with red currant juice.

(*left*)

Glasgow Flip

1 T (2 cl) lemon juice
1 T (2 cl) sugar syrup
1 very fresh egg
ginger ale

1. Put lemon juice, sugar syrup, egg, and ice cubes into a highball glass and mix well.
2. Fill the drink with ginger ale and serve with a straw.

TIP

Flips should not be stirred too long and should not be shaken. They must be served immediately or else they become flaky and unsavory. Make sure the eggs you use are completely fresh!

Orange Egg Nog

1½ oz (4 cl) orange syrup
1 T (2 cl) heavy cream
1 T (2 cl) milk
1 egg

1. Put ice cubes into a shaker and add the ingredients.
2. Cover and shake briefly and vigorously.
3. Strain into a highball glass and serve immediately.

(*right*)

Canaan

5 oz (15 cl) milk
1 egg
2 t honey
cinnamon

1. Shake the milk, egg, and honey without ice briefly and vigorously in a shaker.
2. Strain into a highball glass filled with ice cubes and sprinkle with cinnamon.

TIP

Always mix honey with the other ingredients first, without ice cubes, otherwise it does not combine well.

Bilberry Milk

1 scoop vanilla ice cream
1½ oz (5 cl) blueberry syrup
½ T (1 cl) lemon juice
4 t blueberries
ice-cold milk

1. Put all the ingredients except the milk in a tumbler.
2. Stir, then fill tumbler with milk. (*left*)

Blackberry Shake

1 scoop vanilla ice cream
1¾ oz (50 g) pureed blackberries
1 oz (3 cl) blackberry syrup
½ T (1 cl) lemon juice
ice-cold milk
1 t stiffly beaten whipped cream
chocolate shavings

1. Put the ice cream into a tumbler. Mix the puree, syrup, and lemon juice and pour over the ice cream.
2. Fill the glass with milk and decorate with the whipped cream and the chocolate shavings.
(*center*)

Nightcap

1½ oz (5 cl) hot milk
1 T (2 cl) vanilla syrup
soda water
1 soft caramel candy

1. Mix the hot milk and the vanilla syrup in a tumbler.
2. Fill with soda and attach the caramel candy to the rim of the glass. (*right*)

Tomato Milk

1½ oz (5 cl) tomato juice
1 T (2 cl) lemon juice
1 T (2 cl) buttermilk
ice-cold milk

1. Shake the juices and buttermilk well with ice cubes in the shaker. Strain into a tumbler. Fill with milk. (*left*)

Pineapple Milk

1 scoop pineapple ice cream
1½ oz (4 cl)) pineapple syrup
1 T (2 cl) pineapple juice
½ T (1 cl) lemon juice
ice-cold milk
1 slice of pineapple

1. Put the ice cream into a tumbler. Add the syrup and juice mix.

2. Fill with milk and garnish with the pineapple slice. (*center*)

Pineapple Squash

4 T pineapple slices
3½ oz (10 cl) milk
1½ oz (4 cl) orange juice
½ T (1 cl) lemon juice
1 large scoop of vanilla ice cream
1 T stiffly beaten heavy cream
1 cherry, 1 piece of pineapple

1. Put the pineapple slices into a highball glass. In a measuring glass, mix the milk, sugar, and juices. Pour the mixture over the pineapple.

2. Add the ice cream and decorate with whipped cream and fruit. (*right*)

Almond Coffee

2 scoops of nut ice cream
1 T (2 cl) almond syrup
4 oz (12 cl) cold, strong coffee

Garnish
1 T stiffly beaten heavy cream
toasted almond slivers

1. Put the ice cream into an iced-coffee glass, pour almond syrup and coffee over it and stir briefly.
2. Garnish with whipped cream and sprinkle with almond slivers.
3. Serve the iced coffee with a straw and a bar spoon.
(*left*)

TIP
Serve Almond Coffee with an almond edge. Moisten the edge of the glass with almond syrup, dip the upside-down glass into coarsely ground almonds, and turn it in them slowly. Shake the upside-down glass slightly so the pieces that do not stick fall off.

Iced-Coffee Orange

2 scoops of vanilla ice cream
4 oz (12 cl) cold, strong coffee

Garnish
1 T stiffly beaten whipped cream
1 T (2 cl) orange syrup
chocolate shavings

1. Put the vanilla ice cream into an iced-coffee glass and pour the coffee over it.
2. Place whipped cream on top of it and pour the syrup over it.
3. Sprinkle the iced coffee with chocolate shavings and serve with a straw and a bar spoon.
(right)

TIP
You can make strawberry iced coffee the same way. Use one scoop of vanilla ice cream and one of strawberry; replace the orange syrup with strawberry syrup, and garnish with fresh strawberries.

Mocha Mix

1 t cold mocha or espresso
4 oz (12 cl) ice-cold milk
1 large scoop of chocolate ice cream

1. Shake mocha and milk together vigorously in the shaker.
2. Pour into a highball glass, add the ice cream, and stir briefly.

Index of Recipes

Almond Coffee, 62
American Lemonade, 13
Apricot Fizz, 38
Apricot-Kefir Drink, 50
Apricot Mix, 10
Avalanche, 40
B-Vitamin Milkshake, 52
Babouin, 44
Bahamas, 19
Balear, 34
Banana Mix, 50
Banana Soda, 46
Bavarian Tomato, 27
Berry Freeze, 32
Bicycle, 12
Big Apple, 24
Bilberry Milk, 60
Blackberry Shake, 60
Blood-Orange, 10
Blue Moon, 49
Blushing Virgin, 24
Boston Cooler, 13
Canaan, 58
Caribic, 30
Carlotta, 26
Cherry Kiss, 22
Chocolate-Nut Milk, 57
Chocolate-Orange Drink, 54
Citro Fizz, 23
Citronella, 52
Coco Almond 55
Coco Exotic, 37
Coconut Cocktail, 44
Coconut-Cream Soda, 37
Cola-Mint Cream, 54

El Dorado, 18
Exotic Cup, 24
Glasgow Flip, 58
Granizado of Cassis, 16
Granizado of Lemon, 16
Grape Egg Nog, 58
Iced-Coffee Orange, 62
Jamaica Fruit, 10
Kiba, 52
L'Arbre du Ciel, 36
Lemon Squash, 20
Light Action, 8
Limbo Beat, 29
Magic Drink, 57
Marathon, 9
Miami, 29
Mississippi, 42
Mocha Mix, 62
Nightcap, 60
Olympia Sprint, 9
Orange Egg Nog, 58
Orange Fizz, 23
Orange Lemonade, 42
Orange Milkshake, 49
Paradise, 16
Passion Fruit Freeze, 32
Pear Cocktail, 18
Peppermint Drink, 41
Pincasso, 38
Pineapple Fizz, 38
Pineapple Freeze, 32
Pineapple Milk, 61
Pineapple Squash, 61
Pink Dune, 36
Pirate's Fire, 20

Power Juice, 27
Pyramid, 34
Raspberry Cocktail, 45
Red Butler, 31
Red Cap, 40
Red Currant Creamy, 55
Red Currant Flip, 56
Red Star, 15
Samoa, 34
Saratoga Cooler, 20
Sonny Boy, 50
Strawberry Cup, 14
Strawberry Milkshake, 48
Strawberry Plant, 42
Strawberry Soda, 46
Summer Dream, 14
Sunbreaker, 12
Sunny Coco, 34
Sunrise, 45
Sweet Susie, 46
Tizian, 15
Tomato Cress, 26
Tomato Milk, 61
Tonic Fresh, 22
Triver, 46
Tropical, 28
Tropical Fire, 31
Tropical Sun, 50
Virgin Mary, 26
Vitamin Bomb, 56
Vitamin Milk, 52
William Tell's Shot, 19
Yellow Bird, 16